Sarah Dawson.

GOODBYE SWEET EYE

Tony Weston

Greetings and grateful thanks
to John and Hilary Wakeman
at the SHOp who first took
a few of these poems

and most especially to
MALCOM KERR-MUIR
who plucked out the
offending eye

Published 2015
WINWALOE
99, SOUTH STREET,
BRIDPORT,
DORSET,
DT6 3NZ

ISBN 978 0 9530828 4 1

A catalogue record for this book
is available from the British Library

Printed and bound at the Dorset Press,
Henry Ling Limited,
Dorchester, DT1 1HD

for Felix

CONTENTS

PROLOGUE : NOVEMBER 1ST

There is a problem? This is what I say.
He gently puts his lens down, taps
his fingertips together, tells me, yes,
there appears to be a tumour,
on the ciliary body, comprising
a brown node with an associated
milky-white surround. A cancer?
A melanoma, yes. In a case like this,
he says, looking away, I like to have
a second opinion. Pretending
to be grown-up, I concur.
He shows me, on his model of the eye,
just where it is, this cold-calling visitor.
He reassures me that it can be dealt with,
almost certainly. That Moorfields is the place.
He adds a caveat—I'm not sure if he says
the words aloud— that at the worst
I'll lose the eye. So, I tell myself, you stumble
on a cataract, and tumble into this abyss?

Thin crust of snow. The hollow sound.
The beat of heart. The creak of boot.
The empty air above, beneath.

Lullaby for Felix

The wind is up,
the wind is wild,
the wind has come
for my dear child.

Close the windows,
close the doors,
stuff the cracks
between the floors.

The wind is wild,
the wind is up,
it rattles the saucer
under the cup.

Snuggle up tight,
snuggle up close—
who's the child
I love the most?

NOVEMBER 3RD

Who's that tapping on the glass,
us sat there, counterfeiting normal,
sat there at the kitchen table?
Who's that coming through the door,
eight at night, in winter dark?
Our G.P. come to check us out,
big of frame and big of heart,
he's heard our news and made it his—
a kindness as uncounted on as
a late-home father's kiss.

You're going to be fine, he says.
You're going to be fine— almost
he looks me in the eye.

Nappy-change
for Sophie and Felix

The parcel has come round again.
The playing music holds its breath.
This time, I tell myself, I shall be calm,
I shall not let self-consciousness
fumble my strings. So I unwrap,
my dearest child, your lovely babe and
Lo he smiles! He turns his head away
as though this vision is too bright,
then shyly glances back and beams.
As I undo his babygrow he kicks his legs,
he waves his arms, he weaves his spell—
I know that there is no escape.
I read the entrails as he laughs.
I roll and tab the nappy tight and wipe
and cream his bum, his little elephant.
He thumps his legs against my chest.
His arms go wild. He catches at my thumb.
The heat of him, his glow of skin,
his smell of baking just begun—
I press the button and the music starts.
I wrap the parcel up again. When you return,
with all the day's cares in your head,
he will be ready, for his part, once more
to plant his chuckle in your heart.

SECOND OPINION
NOVEMBER 6TH : CAMBRIDGE LEA

Mr. Newman sees me in the evening.

Like some upmarket airport lounge,
the plush room empties as we encamp
by the water-cooler and a slick machine
which makes you coffee, passable, me
chocolate, good. I wonder what we're doing here?
I want to walk us out into the night,
the chill and natural, untrammelled night.
The secretary at reception's on the twitch. We're last.
I'll check— I think he might have just gone home.
No, no. He bounds in like a distance runner,
lean and fit but with a head that would sit well
on someone fetched from sharpening quills
in a sunlit, high scriptorium. He leaves me whilst
the drops roll back the iris of the eye into its rim.
This time I'm ready with my chin on the machine.
Look at my ear. Look right. Look left. Look up.
Look down. Look back at me. Yes. We both sit back.
A melanoma: treatable, with bracytherapy.
I ask if there is any use in therapies, alternative.
He almost laughs. *Moorfields. John Hungerford's*
your man. Plaque-Therapy. I ask how big a thing?
About 4 mill. It's not a simple shape, but give or take
and growing. You need to have this done.
Firm handshake: he puts his jacket on.

EACH DAY

Each day I put it to the test.
I close the good eye and stare out
the 28 point caps., bold black on white
(for I am full of hope against all hope)
and try to judge how far, how far
the wicked shadow steps aside
and down from every letter on the page.
So, like some calm astronomer, I gauge
a source I cannot see.

I think it grows. I think it grows—
it knows somehow that I am weak.

Songs for a Scubble-mubble
November 13th

Pick up the boy because he's nice,
Cuddle him once and cuddle him twice,
Cuddle him twice and twice times more,
Then throw him up and out of the door.

You're a rascal

You're a rascal,
I'll wrap you in a parcel,
I'll wrap you in a parcel
and send you far away
but it won't do the trick
'cos you're so quick
you'll be back
the very next day.

HOMOEOPATH
For Meenakshi

A gentle goddess this, exhausted, wise,
until, at something foolish that I say,
a sideways, flashing smile knifes out.
Sharp, then, sexy, dangerous— High
Priestess and no doubt a Witch,
abandoned on this cold grey shore
of tiny hard white pebbles where
her craft now rests. Her dark eyes sum me up.
She has my number, makes my remedies

and conjures my shocked soul to calm and peace.

Pulsatilla
November14th

I gave you a pulsatilla,
I said this is just for you.
Yes, I gave you a pulsatilla
And I said this is just for you,
Because you chew,
Because you chew,
Because you chew and chew!

Can you see me Grandpa?

His little hand goes up and grabs
the muslin I have floated on his face.
He yanks it off and burbles with delight.
I cover him again. Again he waits,
then yanks it off and kicks and squeals.
After a few repeats, I change the rules.
I drape the muslin over my old head—

Can you see me, Grandpa? Slowly,
the years are dragged away. He looks
at me, so old and wise, before he laughs.

LOOK AT THE DAYS

Look at the days, see how they fly—
swift as swallows on the wing
gulp the minute and are gone.
Sharp, flitting shadows skip warm ground,
chasing the dreams that are their sun,
breasting the wind in all its ways—
see, how fleet—look at the days.

NEEDS LIVE

Silk-dawn
day-sun
wind-night
lying
awake
until
first-light.

> The leaves
> that fell
> now wet
> with rain.
> Needs live
> with love
> and pain.

Stay and have a beer
November 21st

Tiddle-push, my darling,
Tiddle-push, my dear,
Don't go up to London,
Stay and have a beer,
Stay and have a beer, dear,
Stay and have a beer,
Don't go up to London,
Stay and have a beer.

If he was an apple

If he was an apple
I'd eat him pips and all.
If he was a plum
He'd be gone, gone, gone.
But they've left me a thing
that squeals and dribbles
so I'll just have one
little tiny nibble.

LAST LUCK

If this is last luck, this is the best,
the bit where, with a piece of bread,
you lay down grown-up cutlery
and wipe up all the juice. Though
should they fill my plate again,
I shall fall-to but not forget
this simple time
when I had space to be,
loved by the ones I love
and, in a strange way, free.

PRO-ACTIVE, MY ARSE.
November 22nd

Having heard nothing by the 20th, I ring the NHS.
Sandro at Moorfields is polite but seems obtuse.
They have no letter of referral there. Tight-lipped,
I ask what I'm supposed to do since my consultant
sent his letter on the 6th. I get nowhere with this but
then he tells me, anyway, the soonest Mr. Hungerford
can see me now is in three weeks. When I calm down,
I ring again to book. It takes two days and several calls
to the GP and the Cambridge Lea to sort it out.
Regrettably, it all comes down to my desire for a private
pow-wow with the man. The letter goes to Harley Street
exactly at the point when he removes to Wimpole Street.
I ring nice Sandro to apologise, confirm my date.
I sit and hug today's one coffee to my cheek.
Outside, the wind undoes the last oak-leaves.
To grow, did this thing need the extra weeks?

SORTING THE APPLES

Sorting the apples,
removing the rotten,
setting the boxes again to rights,
seeing the light of grey morning
kissing the golden, brown, black,
souring discards, their skins intact but
bloating, I fetch the camera. It seems I am
needing this insight, this gentle
telling of how all that is, whatever our
yearning is thus on the turn.
No holding it back,
or putting it off,
or taking our time—
nonetheless
taking our time.

For Felix

Let us just say then, let us just say
I am bowled over by this sense of calm,
your quiet grace.

You come like some far visitor
to take our measure, taste our custom
for a space.

Perhaps so many fall like you into this place
on stony ground, are broken, stepped-round
trampled underfoot—

unbearable, the thought. Now, as you sleep,
this Schubert CD playing through your dreams,
let us just say,

let us just say there is such wonder waiting here,
besides warm arms to hold, soft lips to kiss
and babbled messages.

If you are lucky we shall keep it so a good while yet,
until you come into your flower—
until you flower.

DR. WETZLER

A metaphor : we find the wrong bit
of the close in Little Gaddesden.
In the complementary branch, another
fifty yards along the road, behind
a cake-slice pebbled-drive, beyond a Buddha,
a plastic twin-door'd porch without a bell,
stands Dr. Michael, smiling, his quick eye
and handgrip meeting mine. Above
his study door, haloed, by what I take to be
the Star of David, which now resolves
to David's tree, a painting of his younger self?
Laptop, books, a piano with no speck of dust:
haven of calm, of ordered elegance.

My daughter's sent me here to have I.V.
Intravenous vitamin C. This way,
she tells me, as he now confirms, you get
the benefit without the running guts.
He takes a history. He's good at this,
adroit and deft, including Bundle in.
He's complementary not alternative:
confesses to a personal bout of cancer,
in his case bladder, the which, (surprisingly
being ex Bristol Cancer Clinic Medico)
he let them treat with chemo ; just one wash.
Slightly abashed, he sings the virtues of I.V.
laments the FDA stance on B 17. *We used
to do it all the time.* I subsequently learn
a friend was put on trial. Suspended
eighteen months, made sick to death and died.
Drug companies we chime and cross our legs
as one. *The sods are at it all the time — to hell
with what the truth is or who dies, or why,
or who might, with little profit, be made well.*

We stick at vitamin C. and while the drip goes in
I find I'm auditing his age and if, perhaps, we went
to the same North London school. There is
a resonance. We make a second date.
The good Doctor smiles us to his gate.

The Squirgler
November 26th

Unpop all his poppers,
pull off his arms and legs,
put in your nose and ear-plugs—
follow the safety-regs—

and if he tries to fight you,
to squirgle and squiggle away,
pin him down with an elbow
and give him the time of day.

Off with his nappy,
swipe him clean,
send orf a specimen
to the Queen,

pop up his poppers,
stick in his arms,
resist, if you can,
his infinite charms.

THE LADIES' PART—
2, 3, cha, cha, cha

Tonight we're adding to the dance.
She walks us through. She's good,
the soul of patience. What she makes
of all of us, God knows— the skippers,
the clumpers, the all dressed-up, uptight—
but she is kind. She seems to enjoy it.
She is telling us now *the men do their basic,*
the ladies' part is not easy but the men
just do their basic. Ladies, you follow me.
We just do our basic, much confused
by fierce-eyed ladies going sideways,
backwards with a cross, a little cross,
then sideways forward with a turn,
an Alamain turn *that's it ladies,*
Gentlemen, help your ladies with that turn.
It's better with the music but not much.

Later, it's the Rhumba, the dance of love.
Men, behind me. Ladies, I'm doing the men's.
She takes our part. She speaks of hips and men
and shifting weight, of dancing off-the-beat,
the while I'm looking at your face, my love,
so sad, and how you sway your hips so perfectly
and how you look at me from far away
with such command. But will you bear
to look at me, a lead patch on this bloody eye,
when I might up and die? The lady's part's not easy,
no. The lady's part seems, always, difficult.

WINTER FLOWER

And see, it opens like a flower—
the petals of my family, my friends,
the passing touch of folk I barely know,
who know me less but wish me well—
sweet smelling flower I hold you now
against this sad and damaged eye
that it may see the gift of love
it fetches me.

SIGNS AND PORTENTS?

Looking for metaphors, the moon, past full,
is blurred as by a veil of rain, but, with
my good eye only, like a face not yet
quite turned away, half smiling, innocent?

Or take the small, drowned spider in the bowl
that still appeared to walk— was walking
with no air to breathe, against all hope,
that, as the water tipped, scaled my hot hand

and fell the hundred fathoms to the floor
and paused—then crabbed away
between my feet towards the wall. I have
a life to live. I did not wait to see it climb.

O me, O my

O grandson, kicking, waving,
on your sheepskin, on the floor,
how you blissfully revolve.

O fly, frantic beyond all hope,
upended on the window-cill,
how you desperately revolve.

O me, O my, between the two, my
unslept mind, churning the choices—
how you endlessly revolve.

MOORFIELDS: DEC 14
Oncology Clinic 15

A gentle limbo this. Threadbare bucket chairs.
Deserted plastic coffee cups. An air of things
pared down to calm necessity. At odds
a sudden burst of paper-hatted girls erupting
for their Christmas lunch. A quiet again.
Reception is a counter with a tatty cardboard box
that tells me CLOSED— leave your appointment here.
You will be called. A man in shirtsleeves comes
to change the name beside the door. Ah— the clinic,
closed but still in progress through the open doors
was never mine. I am the afternoon. I sit and read,
resigned, a day-old tabloid and find this sadly comforting.
To know what has come next, assists one to be stalled
in this strange, run-down space, waiting to be called…

to ultrasound. Polite, professionally warm,
Sandro walks us up. Ramps everywhere,
more chairs, less bare. A corridor to wait in.
Prints on the wall that would defy halogen
and pristine eyes. We seem like debris
washed-up on a muddy shore. The sea
takes one of us. Each time we're called,
another body comes in on the tide.
Somehow we cluster, make a sort of tribe.
Sighs, smiles are exchanged. As always
at such gatherings I feel a fraud.
There's nothing wrong with me. Just
this damned eye. I should go home.
At last they ask for Weston : Anthony.
I go along to hold his hand. Back by the Clinic
I explore the notes. I see my Treasure Island
marked. Staked out with measurements. Ah!
so the thing Kerr-Muir confided me is real.

The more they squinny in my eye,
with lights and drops and cameras,
the more the day goes on
the less they look me in the eye.
They grow more interested,
intrigued, and more remote.
They leave the clamped-wide ball
firmly in my court.

So , I am making a mountain out of a molehill,
though, to be fair, the molehill is in my right eye,
the nasal quarter and, from that perspective,
its aspect is that of a mountain, gently rumbling.

The Specialist, the Big Man, must think me at best
an infernal nuisance, insisting on being involved.
His perfect plan is to plant a limpet mine, radioactive,
in the anterior position right by the iris, which will,
with luck, roll my mountain on its back, stone dead.

So, I am making a mountain etc. but what if a few cells
crawl away? What if the radiation renders the eye
unfit for use? What if it does not politely pull back
at the retina but makes the odd foray into the brain
aimed as it is at the hypothalamus and my precious
frontal lobe?

        Talking to him, later, on the phone, I sense
his anger. Government Targets! This is his life's work,
vision saving. He's wanting to advance. My Christmas
wish to have the eye out moor and mountain, weak
betrayal, hardly to be borne. His anger shifts to me—
a DIY expert, God help us all! Volcanic man. He has
a point. He's been beleaguered in these mountains years:
his team case-hardened, tired.

        I smile, remembering
their weary shake of heads—*who is this idiot, waving
from his parapet, putting the whole bang-shoot at risk?
What does he want? Does he want to live?*

TIGHTROPE PRACTICE

As though the whole damn circus gawps,
I totter on my practice rope—
and though they're trying to be nice,
mouthing comfort and advice,
and mean it kindly when they say,
Sounds good, must be worth a try—
I saw them hammer in the pegs:
the one end where you lose the eye,
the other where you let them plant
the killer seeds next to the brain
and maybe get away with it.

It's hard to keep one's balance, eh?
To concentrate. You're watching
every step you take, back and forwards,
night and day. Sometimes
you're both feet off the ground,
sometimes six feet beneath.

LOVE SONG TO AN EYE

Now, I'm your advocate—
I've been too slow on your account,
too fraught to listen when you've tried
to tell me. You're tired, you sigh. I'd say,
you're over-wrought. Truth is
you know, you're getting old. Each
time I reassure, placate, advise,
you sink a little more in your esteem,
cave in, let nastiness take hold.

Now, I'm your advocate.
I turn my back and give the nod.

I could not countenance, when all is said,
my murder in your precious bed.

Carol for a Christmas card

Holding him in my arms,
my little Grandson sweet,
I own, though he be such a one,
I would not wish his sacrifice
for all the world.
For all the world
is not enough— so let him be
to dance upon his Grandpa's lap.
The world, god knows,
has had its chance.

The Grand-boy

Before I met this Grand-boy
I never knew, I never thought
a change of nappy could be such
a cause of joy.

Of quiet satisfaction, yes,
like emptying a hoover-bag
without a catastrophic
cloud of dust—

but this Grand Festival
of kicking legs and frantic arms,
of fountains laughingly turned on?
A Carnival

of chuckles, squeaks and shouts,
of eyebrows lifted, faces made
and, at the crucial moment, good
as all get out.

I never thought, I never knew
before this Grand-boy came along
such simple happiness
might be my song.

MINDS MADE UP

Christmas comes and goes.
No word from Moorfields.
We watch the little boy
tear bright paper with strong fists—
a good game this.
We follow a less certain star—
The Big Man has no space for us.
We don't say much.
We hum and haa.

Kerr-Muir is diffident.
He thinks he's not the best,
but finally agrees.
He'll find a spot in January.
His secretary rings us to confirm—
the 5th at Addenbrookes.
Kerr-Muir will enucleate.
Soberly we celebrate.

EYE MINUS 2 : JANUARY 3RD
For Bundle

I hold you close and feel you shake,
like some cold, silver leaf caught in the wind,
with dread of this which soon must come to me.

Embrace it all yourself perhaps you would:
cannot but would, who scarce can bear to take
a needle to your finger for a thorn.

What should I do? I chide. I make
bad jokes as if I simply cannot help myself.
A future pain cannot be halved

but can be doubled. In agony,
you stroke my face and weigh
these precious grams of flesh

against my life. While I stand still
uncomforted and numb,
you hold me knowing that unless—

JANUARY 4TH

1

Tomorrow being my due date—
Now there's a thought— just
as I hoist my daughter's child,
I see that water's coming from above.
Ten minutes gone, the bathroom panel off,
I guess the source: the water-cylinder's gone west.
I drain the system down and gentle life glugs
down the plug. We panic round for plumbers.
Okay for me, I'm off to hospital. My wife
must cope with this. Not fair she's lumbered
but she's stoic and unfazed. Rob from A1
says he'll come. Before we go to bed,
he does. I wake at five and drain the Aga off.
Half-eight I'm bag-packed-on-my-way,
head-down, chin-up into the coming day.

JANUARY 4TH

2

Strange day: a day of being Anthony.
Anthony Weston is he here? Each
waiting-room is full-to-falling-over-feet
with people who look sick as hell—
one man so yellow you can hardly tell
he isn't butter, another with a forehead
radish-red, I guess, from radiotherapy.
Ye gods! Only a sense of duty, which
translates all too soon to apathy,
lets me consent to take a cheese-queue ticket
and just wait. And then I screw it up
and only give the haematologist
one of the clutch of papers in my fist.
in cardiology I realise—and, as I have my ECG
and marvel at these people's tired humanity,
at how they all have asked about my Christmas
as if it mattered for Christ's sake—
I know back there they'll want more blood.
Still, it's not me who has to live with
targets and the endless paperchase.

This Doctor now : a young, delectable,
old-fashionable girl, a Kiwi, eleven long
years from home, this morning learned
her post is being cut. Re-appointed
when she re-applies all well and good—
if not her opthalmology is down the pan.
It makes my loss of eye seem trivial.
The light on the equipment blinks and fails.
She hits it twice. Somehow this says it all.

JANUARY 4TH

3

Dr. Patel is glamorous.
With fragrance-swayed authority
she leads me down the corridor.
She says she will examine me—
and who am I to say her nay?

Only my eye, alas. The drops, the chin on rest,
the lights— *look down, look up, look straight ahead,*
look right, look left. Then Kerr-Muir arrives
more acolytes in tow. The man himself,
as ever courteous, and looking tired to the bone,
requires a careful shufti and, meticulous, enquires
if they might follow suit. Of course, of course.
They call me sir. Must be because their boss
is treating me with overmuch respect.
Or could it be because I'm old enough,
and more, to be their far-off fathers?

First general anaesthetic case I'll be:
nine-thirty in the morning. He tells me
how they have a row of orbs to try for size.
They'll infiltrate the biggest that they can.
He mentions that the Chinese socket is more
nearly round, how the coral (hydroxapatite)
allows blood vessels from the tethered muscles
to grow in. I act a knowing, superficial calm.
He shakes my hand : *see you tomorrow then.*
Not if I see you first. Not if I see you first.

GOODBYE SWEET EYE
January 5TH
6.30 am

Goodbye
sweet Eye.
We both
should cry—

except
it's much
too late
for such.

Your rock-
pool grey
goes out
today.

Look long
and slow—
three hours
to go.

Sweet Eye
goodbye,
sweet Eye
goodbye.

JANUARY 5TH
6.30 pm

Hi there,
old face—
truth is
you're whacked.

Eye bag
beneath
and where
it was

a mound
of fresh
taped
knee pokes

through?
No, the socket
under which
a blind

new ball
swivels
softly sniffing
for the light.

10.00 am

They bring him in to see me,
this babe in arms.
I don't know where to hide myself—
my face of bandages.
He holds his arms out to me
apparently unfazed.
I laugh and smile and speak his happy name—
and want to weep.

11.30 am

The dressing off, I face me eye to eye.
Not quite the man I was, though I can see
the job's as good as anyone could wish:
hardly swollen, barely bruised. Though,
should I sport a patch in gentle company?

Surely I'll have my pick of seats on trains?
A leather jacket, skinhead hair, I'm there—
disco-doorman, drug-enforcer, TV thug.
A new life opens up before the solitary eye.

I don my reading glasses and at once
become just sad and slightly sorrowful.

HOME
January 6TH

This is to be the lucky man, who finds
such greeting of his broken face
as might melt stone. Home warm
and open-armed and friends and family
who call and, bravely, do not turn away.
This thing that is was quite unwished.
I did not seek this travesty,
yet oh, how sweet the mystery
that I, despite myself, am loved.

TO THE OCULARIST

O paint me an eye
as grey as the sea
on an East-coast day.

O paint me an eye
of blue you could drop
and lose in an April sky.

O paint me an eye
of violet to make
the knees of tall girls shake—

No, paint me an eye
Just like my own,
an old string vest
on a mossy stone.

BLIND EYE TURNING

My sister takes my hand and pulls.
She says we're walking in the park,
but there is only close, grey wall.
She pulls me when I say *it's dark.*

My sister tells me to *come on!*
She says I'm lagging far behind,
she calls me from the left, the right,
she says I'm *boring and a fright*

but I am in a tunnel where
I feel the wind but see no light.
I want to curl up in a ball
and dream myself it's only night.

Baby Pie

January 8th

Says Mr. Wimple Wurple-Wup
to Mr. Wimple Wurple-Woo
I've found a juicy baby
but I don't know what to do.

Says Mr. Wimple Wurple-Woo
to Mr. Wimple Wurple-Wup
we'll have a baby pie
and we'll gobble him up.

Says Mr. Wimple Wurple-Wup
to Mr. Wimple Wurple-Woo
if we do that we'll both grow fat
and that will never do.

So, both the Mr. Wimples
walk sadly down the path—
and all that wicked baby does
is kick his legs and laugh.

BEDTIME: JANUARY 8TH

It seems, with good eye closed and earphones on,
I lounge inside a bathroom globe.
A gentle rain runs down the glass.
I feel so calm. At other times, hemmed in by nose,

So, you're disabled now, I think?

this stupid eye seems merely shut,
its lack of openness infuriates.
The good eye closed, there's nothing but
a grey, splotched wall: a stairwell in a tenement—

no stink—so is it still alive?

OF COURSE, THEY MEAN IT KINDLY

The hero in my life, that's what I'd like to be.
A Biggles at the least; even Von Stroheim
with one eye, that would be good. But no,
every second person that we meet has some
known one-eyed wonder—fighter-pilot-racing-
driver-lady-killer—in a patch. I'm left convinced
the heights I need to climb to match such
peerless bastards will be way too much.

I think that I must simply try to be
what I have always found so hard— just me.

Sweet lady

Sweet Lady, in the doorway of my heart,
you shine too bright—no, not for me—
for me you light my every stumbling step,
your burning filament my guiding star,
but now, for pity of yourself, stretch out,
stretch out and dim the inner switch, before
my eye, dear love, grows used to it.

Dear love, my eye grows used to it.

You're a Pirate

You're a little Pirate,
you're a Buccaneer—
you poke my eye
and you pull my ear
you swig my tea,
you finger my curry,
but don't you worry
I'm in no hurry—
I eat pirates by the dozen,
I make pirates disappear!

You're my treasure
you're my jewel,
you're my secret
rocket fuel—
strike your match
on my rough heart,
rend the cloudy skies
apart.

Finding the socket vacant, boarded-up,
a fat red grape has seen its chance
and aims, it seems, at squatter's rights.
Blindly, it's trying all the moves:
it emulates the neighbour day and night.
It weeps a lot as if some ænome,
some yearning for a hillside in the sun,
for coffee-girls or garlic-boys
kept it from joying in the ways
of baby-wipes, eyedrops and being in
the lap of homoeopathy.
I wish it well. I want it to fit in. It might,
for me, just peek next door
and dress itself in grubby grey and white.
This would be neighbourly.

I found

I found this little squirrel,
I dressed him all in blue,
I put him in a treetop,
I thought I'd start a zoo
But all the other animals
Just upped and ran away —
So I coaxed him down again
And here he is today.

I found this little turnip,
I dressed him all in cream
I bought myself a fishing-rod,
And dropped him in the stream
But he refused to take my bait
And sank just like a stone —
So I dried him on a towel
And lent him my best comb.

I found this little mussel,
I dressed him all in black
And heated up the water
For a juicy little snack,
But he squiggled and he giggled
And he quite escaped my hand —
O, why does nothing ever
Go quite the way you planned?

I found this little radish
And I dressed it all in red
And went to gather salad,
When the thought came in my head
That it looked just like a baby
On the green and leafy plate—
So I swore I would adopt it
Before it was too late.

DOMESTIC INTERIOR

I slice the bread. You turn the toast.
We pass the Marmite. We are most
comforted by this
unambitious bliss.

The dark comes down. It fetches rain.
I wipe my eye. There's little pain.
A cup of tea,
would you agree,

another slice, on such a night
outclasses many grand delights?
I touch your hand.
You understand?

WHEN I GET MY GOOD EYE
January 16th

When I get my good eye,
The one that cannot see,
Then I shall go upon the Town —
There'll be no stopping me.
> *For who can wear an eye-patch*
> *And not give girls the eye?*
Yes, I shall wear an eye-patch
For the glamour that it lends
And I shall pass the pretty girls
Stood chatting with their friends,
> *For who can wear an eye-patch*
> *And not give girls the eye?*
And when they cluster round me
And ask me what the war?
Then I will lift my eye-patch
And they will wonder more
> *O who can wear an eye-patch*
> *And not give girls the eye?*
Then I shall speak of wondrous powers
Attaching to this eye:
That it can see into their breasts
And far beyond the sky
> *For who can wear an eye-patch*
> *And not give girls the eye?*
Then I shall up and take my leave,
Yes, leave them all a-quiver,
For with a glad eye or without
I doubt I can deliver.

LANDLORD'S LAMENT
January 17TH

I crouch against my pillowed wall
to lick my wounds— or would, but friends,
acquaintance call to wish me well,
to see quite how I hurt and mend.

No sooner is the phone put down, it rings.
God, yesterday was trial enough—
old cooker out, new cooker in,
new bathroom globe, new basin taps—

but now the stopcock's dripping
in that damn rental house. It lurks
behind the cupboard by the sink and thinks
because I'm half-way blind I'll blink—

and then it comes to me. The Universe
is telling me the game's not up:
won't let me curl against the wall
but tugs my hand and hauls me up.

CONSEQUENCE
January 18TH

A fool to himself, you'll say: bedtime,
checking the gilded gules of the eye,
under the temporary clear-plastic shield
I see a pear shaped lump of snot?
About the size of a sixth of the iris
were it still there. Downstairs, I sit
at the kitchen table. I think. I dowse.
I ask the pendulum *is this ok?*
No. *Is this cancer?* No. *Is this
an infection?* Yes. *Should I leave this
to the medics or should I do my stuff?*
No and yes.
                    So—stiffen-up the sinews,
out with the conformer, mimicking,
as best I can Kerr-Muir's deft technique.
The thing's not round but ovoid
with a squared-off wing: more curved
than you'd expect. I rinse it off. I flood
the raw eye with official eye-drops, which
don't sting : the coral eyeball rough
and bloody as a battered steak—
how can this be? I put the 'shell'
back in, then wonder is it upside down?
I leave it be and take two ibuprofen,
not so much for pain as for the comforting:
they help me sleep, though not tonight—
for here I am, at this same table, scribbling.

53

Sophie

How does she manage it all, this daughter of mine,
her house, her work, her dog, her lovely child,
her wounded dad?

And being ill beside:
this stupid, self-defeating thing that half
the doctors laugh away as all-in-the-mind.

I wish sometimes she'd let me scoop her up
to sing and cuddle her asleep
as once I could,

but now it's all
the other way, or mostly so. She
cossets me and spends her strength and lends

her perfect little boy with all the joy he brings—
ah, what a magic thing his openness,
his brightening.

LAST NIGHT I DREAMED A FUNERAL?

After the Terrible Thing, the Great Disaster,
we are all filing out into the street.
It is time. I know, for some reason,
though nothing is said, for me to speak.
We line grey tarmac either side. Twin strips
of scrubby grass. My mind a blank,
I squint into the sinking sun.
I raise my hand. The words begin—

With the sun in our eyes we cannot see
those who stand on the other side.
Sometimes we hardly believe they are there.
We ache for a friendly cry, a familiar curse.
Could we just step over—something forbids us.
We try to remember and the trying drives
the touch of their hands only farther away.
So, let us not think. Let us go. Let go.
Let us be glad we can feel the sun
on our faces. Let us hope they feel
the warmth of the sun on their backs,
leaning their shadows long towards us.

THORN

In the far Americas, these Wise Men say,
the World and everything that therein is
was made five thousand years ago—
and they explain the way our universe expands
by positing a somewhat quicker speed of light.
Maybe they're right,
or anyway as right
as what my right eye swears is gospel truth :
that all the world's a flat, grey wall
which lacks a floor and wants a roof.
I wouldn't know. The simplest thing
is hard to find. A pair of sharp eyes
is a boon, one sharp eye is a thorn.

ONE O'CLOCK: ALL'S NOT WELL
January 25TH

So, here I am, again, drinking water,
eating chocolate, making a magic pendulum
because the other is besides my darling's bed.
A lump. Under the arm. Not big. Pea-sized —
but *little acorns* spring to mind. Now, I dowse.
Not cancer, no. Not lymph. A sweat gland? Yes.
Just what I want to hear? Of course. I made this
pendulum to give the answers, didn't I?

The chocolate, at least, has made me calm.
To tomorrow's list I add *buy smoothie-maker*.
Round the spoiled globe the starving kill for bread.
I sit and poke my little, failing fire of private dread.

January 26th

I have an entertaining hat,
It's pink and warm and rather fat.
It squeals and laughs and waves its arms—
I wonder, should I be alarmed?

O, quick, quick— quicker than quick,
I think it's going to be sick !

January 27th

Put him in an Orphanage,
sell him off for tripe.
Put him in an Orphanage,
he's getting rather ripe.

We might have sold the baby
but where would be the point?
Put him in an Orphanage
and sit and have a joint.

O, put him in an Orphanage etc.

LAST APPLES
January 28TH

The favoured knife explores the skin, the still white flesh.
It glides then gouges deep beyond the brown, the rot.
Eyeball after eyeball, quartered, sliced, put on to boil.
Rising, a roiling foam subsumes identity,
leaves now a woven, subtled mash of memories,
of shape of bud, of flower, of dancing leaf.
Soft salvage, soon to solace as we eat
with sweet, autumnal stored up heat.

A BUCKETED CLOWN
January 29TH

Each waking-up the optic nerve
behind the false-eye credits light—
or is it that the brain expects
each eye to do its duty? Either way
it brings a comedy of some confusion,
confounding the bright motes and beams
on which the sister eye still dotes.

But shut the lid or don a patch
and all comes clear. If not it's
blunder down like some old bear,
head stuck in an empty honey-jar—
like a tripped and bucketed clown.

DAY AND NIGHT
February 3RD

Behind the lino-cut of trees,
there, where the fox barks, where the owls
make mockery of tucked-up men,
O, sad, thumb-sucking, fucked-up men,
whose duveted dreams are dragged by howls
beyond the cut-out line of trees
into the one-eye of the Moon—

come morning, bright as polished brass,
when once the frost is rubbed away,
picked-out with snowdrop, aconite,
and these presenting debutantes,
these hellebores all curtsey and display—
comes morning, bright as polished brass
beneath the one-eye of the Sun.

TENNIS

Second time out I'm playing not so well.
I fancy it's because I know it's possible
to hit the ball

and so I miss.
Though it gets better as the sleety rain
sweeps down across the fields into our game.

We play on, being past our prime and daft.
We end up soaked and frozen to the bone.
We shake our heads.

We stand and chat
as if we think we should. *Not half-bad—you
played a blinder*— there's half-a-beat before we laugh.

FEBRUARY 9th

The time of the year when the oil runs out,
when the pendulum stops,
when the fog comes down like a grubby cloth—

little boy kicking and shouting for joy.

The time of day when the dark clumps in
and stamps its mud across the heart
and swears and knocks your smile about—

little boy kicking and shouting for joy

bright as an ember in the draught.
Kneel by him now, scrumple your fears,
stack them about him, sing to the fire—

little boy kicking and shouting for joy
little boy kicking and shouting for joy.

Snowmelt

For Roger and his Alison
February 11th

Snowmelt: the field more splash than grass,
odd jewels of sorrel leaves burned garnet by the frost.
Your birthday, then: buds in the roses, hazels rich
with catkins, seeming none the worse. Such
treasure still on this bedevilled earth,
such cause for joy and gentle grief
that you are gone, no more to share it with.

TOMORROW AND TOMORROW
February 11TH

The eye, does it heal well? Too slow,
or, as I fear too quick? God knows.
Two days yet to the consultation.

 Prised wide, the eyelids show a slide of flesh
which leaves clear plastic staring bright—
strange sliver of ham inside and out.

Growing from where? Where is there but where
muscles mesh with coral eyeball? No other thought
presents itself. I let the eyelids gently fall.

Mirror, mirror on the wall who is the weirdest
of them all? Come on, it's not too bad.
One red eye, iris oval, eau-de-nil,

a coral reef as yet undrowned by rising flesh?
I rub the bone above the eye to ease the pain.
Tomorrow and tomorrow all shall be explained.

CLINIC 3
February 12th

The clerk demands to know if I am recent:
have my details changed? I tell her *yes* and *no*.
We solemnly agree on my address.
I have a sudden vision: waiting-rooms
across the land combined in one, a mile
high pile of tatty magazines for all
the patient multitude, a giant bin replete
with plastic cups, a plastic waterfall
iced against the all pervasive warm.
I come to earth. I sit. My name is called.
The ritual reading of the card.
Put your hand over your left eye and read
for me the lowest line you can. I laugh.
I'll have a go. She stares at me, then checks
her list—and reddens. *The left eye only then.*
I struggle with the bottom line. *Thank you,*
she says, *if you'll just take a seat again.*
Chastened, I find myself another magazine.
Time settles like a fine, grey dust. Disturbed
by each small to and fro, the seconds lift
and float, re-settling layer on sifted layer.
Not long before I see a Mr. Achar: young, urbane.
From his brief look I gather something's wrong.
Kerr-Muir confirms. No coral should be visible:
the stitches holding the conjunctiva have gone.
A set-back merely but it means a general
and a month or more delay. I kick myself.
I should have listened to my ignorance.
It sensed something not right a month ago.
A queued-for coffee in the concourse : slow, slow—

but talking with a student-midwife whom we know,
mother of a teen, gone bravely back into the flow,

today assigned to A&E (although no one had told them so)
finds herself sent-off to have another coffee: de trop
and useless— so, what's a broken stitch or two?

Back home, I light the Aga, since the oil has come.
It takes first go: the shields begin to softly glow.
In this, at least, they're sensible and kind, the Gods,
as they are not to half, half-blind Mankind.

February 13th

First you nibble a foot,
Then you nibble another,
Then you gobble him up—
But you don't tell his beautiful mother!

Next you nibble a hand,
Then you nibble another,
Then you gobble him up—
But you don't tell his beautiful mother!

Next you nibble an ear, etc.

Next you nibble a cheek, etc.

Next you nibble a nose,
What a shame he hasn't another—
I blame his beautiful mother!

DRIVING MORE SLOWLY
February 14th

Crab-apples rotting by the road, beyond which
clippings of leylandii have killed the grass
and probably the violets. A sodden, solitary hawk,
a score of magpies, more. By the piled manure
seven, I think— for a secret never to be told,
which is, perhaps, that this becoming old
is tenable if you can beat your brambled way
back through the wood to where and when
your young heart dances to the beat, your soul still
stepping with a skip. Stand in the doorway. Make
no sound. Shake off the years of carried dust,
write on the varnished table where you, vacant, sit—
O TAKE DELIGHT, DELIGHT IN THIS .

SQUARE ONE
February 15th

1

Mr. Woodruff takes me firmly by the mind.
He's like an arrow ready strung.
Look up, look down, left, right. Sits back.
I think—we need to start again.
I think we need a smaller orb.
The conjunctiva is delicate. It's thin—
the orb is spiky, like a hedgehog.
When you try to drag it back across—
I demur. I tell him how it floated
on the eyedrops neat, apparently intact
when I removed the shield, three weeks ago.
He's not impressed. I try to state, as fact,
the muscles have grown in now, surely—
Not really, yet. I hear the arrow sing.
You come in Friday at 7.30. Yes, first thing:
you'll be first one on my list. I could be wrong.
We'll take a good look then, though, in your long
term interest, I think a fresh start would be best.

2

I'm back to a summer afternoon, oh, years ago.
Set-out in the sun, to dry from raw-glazing,
half a kiln-load of pots on boards on a ladder,
the ladder balanced on an upturned plastic bin—
casseroles, coffee-pots, jugs, mugs, a breadcrock—
looking good. Stepping away, cup of tea in my fist,
at my eye's corner the too-warm plastic gives,
the ladder tips and everything slow-motion slips
onto the grass. A weeks work gone, in a moment.
This isn't like that: not a total disaster. The cancer's

not spread. We're talking a month or two's setback.
This is more like hefting a wet jug, just thrown
still on its bat, out through the doorway into the sun,
catching its lip on the door-jamb. Standing, cursing,
turning, knocking the clay back into a ball.
Wedging and throwing, from scratch, again.

FOSTERING SALOME
February 16th 8 am.

Five weeks ago they gave this one to me.
I did my best to break the ice,
but not a peep.

Took time, but now we've settled down:
no longer scared to make a move,
no longer on the twitch.

Sometimes, at night, when we are both asleep,
I sense this wild, abandoned dance,
this singing thing.

And here she comes, all silken scarves : no
colours, just these glorious, weaving
greys, wafting away.

O Salome, O Salome! My head is sore,
my blood runs in the tray. It should be so—
such pretty flesh is not for show.

They tell me now she'll have to go.
the damage is irreparable. God, I'll miss
the clever, sexy little sod.

FALSE START
8.10 am : February 16th

The anaesthetist comes bouncing in to tick the boxes—
(the nice nurses have already done this twice)
On any medication, history of illness, any allergies—
No intravenous mushrooms, then? You're down
half-eight—first off the blocks. Any worries?
Eight-twenty and he's back. *I told you wrong,*
you're second up, Ok? See you then, about ten.
I fill the time. Outside, the sun is doing early-rounds,
but here, our curtains are all drawn. It wouldn't do
to have him poking in and altering things.
We're not his specialty, or his concern.
He might just want us in the open-air
and tell us to breathe deep and get a grip.
We take a different line in here. I do
another small, precautionary pee, then
mosey back and make a call or two.
Just ansaphones. I blank the screen. I'm best alone.

Mr. Woodruff jolts me into real space.
He takes me through the options once again.
We'll open up and take a look. If there's enough—
he closes thick, pink curtains in the air—
for a repair that's what we'll do: less work for me.
If not we'll start again but with a smaller ball.
He ticks me through the multiple-choice:
more like the menu of the day than my
required consent. I see, with some alarm, that fat
may be extracted from elsewhere to pad, should it
be needed, any little sag. *It's most unlikely,* as he ticks.
If I were on a field of war, I'd want this man
right next to me. I sign and print. He shakes
and sprints. *See you at ten— or thereabouts.*

At last we're on our way. The same anaesthetist,
all Aussie spin and charm but strangely pale
despite the slow left arm, remarks the NHS
no longer gives them tourniquets, so makes one
from a latex glove and fits the shunt. Nice work,
I say. He spills the drip all down my arm.

Come-to and know the ball is changed.
Something lost and something gained, I hope.
Dopey still, but try to phone my lovely girls.
This hopeless fancy screen reports I'm out of funds.
No techno-phobe: drugged and incompetent, perhaps,
but even I can spot a money-screwer laughing
in my plastered face. A nice nurse comes to tell me
that you've phoned and will be in at two. Can't believe
how much this means. I'm quite redundant with relief.

Simon Woodruff, looking younger by the hour.
(did he drink my virgin blood?) He 'fesses-up':
he did the deed. Somehow, I always knew he would
and, by the feel of it, he's done it well.
He finds me on my feet en-passant to the loo.
So, you'll be going home today. I shake his hand
I smile. I can, no really can forgive him everything.

Kerr-Muir next. I take it kindly that he's come.
He tells me he was there some of the op.
I don't know how he found the time. His list,
as ever, was chock-full. He's just that sort of man.
All your good work, I say, I'm feeling bad.
He shrugs, admits to disappointment, yes —
but thinks it all went very well: a good result.
Then, he thanks me for the poems: how moved
he was and how they get no feed-back as a rule.
He smiles, a little sadly and puts out his hand.

HOME AGAIN
February 18th: 6.30 am

This time I'm told to leave the pressure-pad
an extra day.
Flesh at the edges swells, subsides and swells
with the delay.

The eyebrow hairs grow more attached.
This plaster's here to stay.
I gently work the edges. She catches me.
I'm told *don't play* —

What's underneath I hardly want to see.
I wouldn't say
it's easier this time, but soon I'll close
the other eye and pray —

and when I do, it's both hands on and rip.
Surprisingly, it doesn't hurt at all.
The eye looks sad and somewhat small,
cornered, like something animal,

exhausted, backed against a wall.
Extending a slow, soothing hand,
I tenderly unseem the sticky lid —
baleful, red and hunkered down,

but doing quite nicely, so it seems:
a kiln just past the critical degree,
its cooling glow a dull cerise.
I lower the lid: I put the bung back in.

ABOVE THE DIN
February 18th

The past three years
Three friends have died.
So many more are sick.
So many live suspended in
some thrash of fearful hope.
It seems so few enjoy
the living they now muddle through.

In our small corner
of this gathering we sit
to hear the numbers called
in a raffle no one wants to win.
Did any of us think
that we were buying into this?
We drink, we joke above the din.

FEBRUARY 19TH

1

These mornings when the geese skate by
casting their cries of fly with me—
scribing by artificial light,
the backward print of poems bleeding through,
making small sense of what I scrawled last night—
I feel my wings ache and my feathers itch
and tip the good eye quick to catch
the glint of grassbound water far beneath.

2

Finding his language thin, the hang-dog
pale vocabulary, the tattered bits of cliché
dragged along and his persistent sin
of saying nothing new and little wise,
he nonetheless takes comfort in
the blithe outsendings of his butchered eye—
grey patterns, rich as blood-trayed marbling.
Waking from dreams of colour he begins
to notice how his daily stint is patterned grey
with beauties fit to clothe a prince.

I'm getting to expect the shadow at my shoulder,
silently, off-puttingly, leaning in that bit too close.

A fellow trainee in the GLC, blond hair and pimples,
in his green suit, would stand just so and quietly loom
as I concocted site reports. He meant no harm,
just had no sense of personal space. It drove me wild.
When I exploded, told him what I thought
he backed away bewildered, sad-eyed, hurt.

So, in these latter days, I humour this, unwelcome
as it is—except when going out in company or driving
in the car. Then I assume a charming patch and an
insouciant air to mask the prickle lurking there.

Coldy Felix
February 20th

Today, he rattles as he bounces, little lungs
flock-full of phlegm, but squeaks and chuckles still
when hoisted to the mirror, reaching out to touch
his eager chum. I lower him. He juts his little chin
like Popeye, coughs, then growls in imitation
of the cat and then he's up and bouncing with a will,
doing his level best with how he is— and how he is
is wonderful, despite this bug. He stops mid-bounce
and stretches out a soft, splayed hand toward my eye.
Gently, I say. He looks away. Then looks again.
He leans his little nose to mine. Sublime. Divine.

CLINIC 1
Newmarket

Like someone to avoid because their tears
come at the call of any kindly touch,
Newmarket always seems about to rain.

We find the Hospital. We park outside,
although the web-site stated we could not.
Inside, out of the spittle of the wind,
I make a sidelong dash into the loo.
Despite we're early, I'm already called:
Mr.Woodruff has not heard of waiting lists.
The statutory reading of the chart— my all-
night in and out of sleep now means the eye
refuses to perform— yes, that's the bottom line.
Young Simon, jolly here, relaxed, seems
pleased to see me and my twice-times eye,
which follows his raised biro like a dog.
He gives us both a little pat and says
five weeks before the prosthestist, three
months before I get my personal eye, which
will be light but might, in years to come,
necessitate a very minor lift. He shows me
on his own unflagging eye: the customised
but unaccustomed weight, alas
may drag my ageing beauty down.
We lightly touch on decimated flora: how
antibiotics may make you sick.
His goodbye grip dismisses you and this.

It's drive off, gladly, into town. A coffee
(Premier Travel) then it's off like hounds
through the Hospice, Heart Foundation
and the Cancer Campaign shops.

Felix and Sophie

February 23rd : 3.50 am

Fast, on his side, your baby sleeps.
Safe in its double keep of fired clay
the candle burns half-down. Clouds,
stooping to this flawless scene,
flecks the velux glass with rain.
Relaxed, I tread upstairs again
to bed. Your gentle snore arrests
me on the landing and attests
that we, in staying you beneath
our roof, are doubly blessed.

For Felix or for Grandpa?

See— iridescent, clear
glass bubbles, silver in the candlelight,
their cheating web of lines invisible—
dancing, at my touch, for your delight.
Little chap, you lie, arms stiff with ecstasy,
head cushioned on your muslin, hands
fisted now, now starfish wide. You squeak.

Three Christmases ago I put these up.
I had no way to know that, so, I'd sit—
my heart against the table edge,
my arms under these thrashing legs,
seeing this magic through your eyes,
sharing such unencumbered sight—
such borrowed joying to confess.

THIS MOMENT
February 24TH

Power-cuts I used to love; prided myself
in stepping careless through the dark,
hand out exactly to the shelf
on which the box of matches stood.
Feeling smug, I'd then retreat
across the kitchen and the hall
into the cupboard where the candles live.
Could do this with my eyes shut, so I thought—

but this moment, would I be elsewhere?

Now, in the half-light of a winter's dawn,
the cautious half-sight of wide-open eye,
I cross the kitchen, touching chair to chair,
so not to wake you, sleeping still
above my head. I calculate each move I make
like some forsaken astronaut adrift in near despair
against the blind side of the moon, skills pushed
to last ditch limit of arms-length repair—

but, this moment, would I be elsewhere?

ALL TOLD
February 26TH

This morning wasn't good. My
seeing-eye too tired to concentrate,
its dumbly unrepentant mate
doing its best to help. I'm glad
you couldn't see me fool and faff,
my pool of milk beside the cup,
and just how gracefully I swept the pile
of papers off the corner of the kitchen table.
Can anybody tell me? No matter how we try
there's always too much stuff on every surface
in the house. Tidying has never worked for us.
Then me, attempting to feed lead into my pencil—
symbolic failure this, not calculated to enhance
my sense of being man-still-managing.

This morning wasn't bad. The lumps
under the other arm are going down, the last
of those damned antibiotics done. I'm glad
I didn't panic and rush off to hospital.
The mended eye looks happier, albeit shy.
You seem no longer quite so mad at me
and in the spread of papers on the floor
was something I had long been searching for.
I wrote another poem about Rog.
I did a bit on Riddley for your class.
We had a go at tennis and improved
despite the wind, despite the cold.
despite the simply getting old.
This morning wasn't bad, all told.

Felix and Grandpa

February 27th

I pick you up and hold you to the glass:
Felix and Grandpa, there they are! You laugh.
You pat the glass and rest one hand on me,
one hand on where we snuggle, cheek to cheek.

I take you through to change and as I do,
swiping you clean, putting on your cream,
the thumb goes in the mouth. I zip
the yellow sleeping bag, turn on the music,

gently nudge the Teddy who lives here
into your neck. Your eyes are closing
as I step away. Is this the moment when
I ought to stop the film and end the show?

Instead, I call the writers in. I say —
look, if we're doing this full-length,
please, look me in the eye and promise me,
whatever stuff you put these people through,
you'll somehow find a way to hold on to
this thing they have, the old man and the boy.

A SOCIAL THING
February 27th

Courage, it seems, still must be learned.
It's up the iron steps, pushed from behind.
Big girls and boys have gone before.

To turn and fight your way back down to earth,
to duck the friendly blows, the frightened jeers,
requires a touch of more

than simple nerve. Surely all must take their turn,
their medicine—chemo, radiotherapy? It's only fair.
But what you want to know

is does it hurt and will it work? Brave friends
have climbed and launched and gone to ground.
So, though it has a pull,

this dreadful slide of dubious chemistry,
this kill or cure philosophy, is not for me.
Bravado's just a social thing.

Letting go
For Bundle and her mother

Tense, but tactful, with my one-eyed driving,
you quietly say *I had forgotten this*
as we turn left beneath the blue-brick bridge.
Ah yes, we are about to come upon
the friendly crematorium so helpful
when your mother died one year ago today.
Untypically last night you didn't sleep for
thinking back how, after dancing, you had said
we must go, now, to Margaret House.
Well, sweetheart, you were there to catch
and coax away her fear. Stroking her face,
you told her calmly that she'd been so good.
You soothed her sleepwards like a fretful child
and gave her currency to cross: for letting go.

Next day, your birthday, you went twice.
She died between: slipped sideways through
the flimsy curtains of the mind and out
into a place I see as full of light and flowers.
Your absence from her going troubles you:
good daughters, surely, do not grudge the hours?
We pass the gates. I wish I could do more.
I close my fingers lightly round your wrist.

Perhaps she sensed you'd tether her,
against her will, against your own, with hold
of hand so like her own. Involuntary grasp
of love, you'd think, but this she never knew
quite how to show to one as different as you.

WORKING BY EYE
March 1st

Three hours graft, I'm aching for my bed.
Clearing floor-space, bench-room, shifting
and de-nailing wood.

Out with the skil-saw, jigsaw, plane;
the beading-tool made fit to do its bit again,
the aromatic reek

of rescued pine. The juggling round the splits,
the buried nails, the too-bad edge of worm—
working by eye.

Appreciating now, before each move I make,
I need to suss things with my fingertips.
Poor execution

of some simple kitchen shelves: shaming,
but a triumph nonetheless. The cradle gift
of double vision,

lost as any screw dropped in the shavings
and the dust, I know I shall not find again,
yet grateful,

any-which-way to go on, waking, as needs must,
into each half-dark yawning, disbelieving
gift of morning.

MEENA : HOMOEOPATH
March 2nd

And how are you, again she asks? Ok, I lie.
She steeples hands in greeting to the gods,
let's do some healing then, she smiles
and, as she chants her people round, I close
my half-shut eyes and feel it sweeping in
as on a weather chart, not serious, not
hurricanes or floods or freezing fog,
a ridge of slightly narrowed isobars
across the flat soul's waiting hinterland.
This depression, says the smiling weather-girl,
looks set to last for several shallow years.

Saint Winnal's Day

March 3rd
for Roger Deakin's friends

Back to the pillowed wall, sat on the bed
upstairs and listening to the darkening rain,
I think of how we laughed and what was said.
Hard rain that ticked repeatedly the windscreen
on the good drive home into the sunset's
startling show: great anvils climbing high behind
stark piles of pristine cauliflower, iconic gilding
lavishly laid on against forbidding lip
of purple slate subsumed in breast of dove —
the whole thing overdone. For certain all
of you are now long back from the walk you took
with Roger in your heads. Well, and did you revel
in the sky's slow Turnering, seeing those Philistines,
the rooks scoot in all scold and jostling, or did
you talk and puzzle more what should be done —

or turn our lost friend's way and let him point
each startling thing you might have missed?

Felix : almost 8 months

1

He'll wake at ten or thereabouts,
his mother says—he'll let you know—
and so he does, though not by yells
but rather by some psychic pull
which has me peeking round the door
to see him wide-eyed on his mother's bed,
Heartsease the cat curled at his feet
and such a smile for me I'm utterly beguiled.

I sit and stroke your face, you catch my hand
I lower my face until it lies at anchor
next to yours. You gently press your fist
against my cheek. I find I cannot speak.

2

Cover him in pastry,
go and have a shower,
put him in the Aga,
leave him for an hour,
drizzle him with lemon sauce,
pop a mouthful in—

sure, to leave the smallest scrap
would be a mortal sin.

MARCH 11TH

Like going too long without a pee, self-pity burns,
self-pity hurts and, though it brings relief,
also disgusts. One shakes oneself. One turns away.

Come on. What once was possible may still be so,
given the fine facilities of car and house,
felicities of family and friends, of loving spouse —

though every step along the way recalls
the shuffling walk of old men once stepped round.
My eye-patch rings me like a leper's bell.

Ah, yes, each day gets easier as I learn half-blind
and, yes each day gets harder too, a wary
closing fist behind the windows of my mind.

Perhaps, when I can counterfeit two eyes,
when I am looking something more myself
I shall reach down leftover purpose from the shelf?
Meanwhile, I shake myself. I turn away.

Well

Well, look at this baby
I think I've found—
He was lying about
On the dirty ground.

If we clean him a little,
If we clean him a lot
He'll probably be
The best baby we've got.

High-chair show

I show you Mr. Punch.
I show you how he throws
the baby up and makes it cry.
Drink firm in little fist,
from your high-chair,
you look on nonplussed.
I make him *kissy, kissy, kiss*.
You laugh at this—
I do not do the bit where
the Daddy drops the child.

LETTING THE CHICKENS OUT
March 14th

Staggering down in my dressing-gown,
the sun leaping-up and licking my eye
I see, through the blear, a sky of a blue
all but vestals should eschew. Though rheum
lies still in the meadow beyond the stretching
ring of silent trees, here plum-blossom sings
in the charcoaled arcs of Spring's first sketch.
With merry squawks, the hens bounce brisk
from the ramp in run-and-search. Alas, no eggs.
I stand and pee on the troublesome whiff of fox.
My good eye laughs at the shrinking frost.
The libation splashes my wellington boots.
The cold, sharp answering breath of waking
earth raises the hair on my bare old legs.

MARCH 18TH
2.00 am

A night of simple aches and pains,
brought on by nothing worse than age—
there's nothing worse than age—
it comes at you remorselessly
as Cillit-bang.

You mute the sound: horror contained
by your remote, two nurofen, a cup of tea.
Sore-eyed, you read a book till three.
You rotate pillows uselessly:
still feel all wrong.

With growing light it starts to rain.
You tell yourself this should engage
your sympathy for those out-wild,
hopelessly uncomforted,
drifting and undone.

To see her now

This headstrong girl, this child of mine—
so bright and weary, like a candle flame
that gutters in the door's sly draught,
that bends and gutters but will not go out,
will not give in to pain or pain's despair—
I love her so, this headlong girl,
I ache for her, this child of mine.
To see her now with her dear child,
his little arms held out, their locking smiles.
To see her tend him, greet each need
with gentle laughter and deft wiles.
How pleased they are, each one with each.
How far beyond the reach of words
this love so spoken without speech.

All night you've been awake with him
in fits and starts, in coughs and pukes,
yet, patiently, you let him play
pulling your glass of lemoned water
to his lips, then pushing it away.
Delighted with his joke he laughs.
You laugh to see him breathing free.
Enfolded in your being's loving cloak,
he chuckles at your kind caress,
rejoicing in his little wickedness.

Two minds
March 18th

Day of a divided mind: bright sun,
cold wind and hail strewn thick as sugar lumps
spilled from a giant Tate & Lyle.

Tail tucked, my daughter's bouncy dog,
who paddles happily chest deep in winter streams,
comes hurtling-in in high alarm.

Indoors, the baby rolls and kicks in circles
on the play-pen floor and squeaks and shouts
in high delight as we three laugh.

Thinking it almost stopped, I put the dog
and basket in her car—responding as I always do—
we're doing this? Let's do it then.

Felix, the teething, happy boy removes his hat
to greet the sky's unwelcome chill, wet kiss.
I strap him in and wrap him round.

My daughter tells me to go in. Go in. Not being
clever at goodbyes, I turn away. I hear the engine start
with clutch and lift of a divided heart.

A splendid find

Well, there's this baby in a pram—
I thought now here's a find.
It chuckled as I picked it up,
it didn't seem to mind.

I fed it up on raspberries
and marmite in hot gin:
and not a word of mother's milk—
and where would one begin?

I let it crawl about the house.
It's eager to explore.
It smells a bit of something else,
I prop it by the door—

which means I have to be alert
to what is going on.
It's easy to forget oneself—
and then your baby's gone.

TO THE LITTLE BOY IN THE STREET
and Pirates everywhere

You hove in view, yesterday,
dragging a bit on your Nanna's hand,
on the way to the shops

and, seeing my eye-patch, facing
a real, live Pirate, you blurt it out
then scuttle for cover.

As we draw level, I scowl
and give you my best growl, broadside—
Aah— aarrrrgh! You squeal

with delicious fright.
Your Nan, giggling, grapples you close,
did you see that? She asks.

Well satisfied, one and all,
with our plunder, we haul-away
into our harbouring lives,

you, half-believing in Pirates,
me, half, in little boys. Nannas,
of course, we all believe in.

AUTO-PORTRAIT
March 22nd

He longed for happiness to shake him like a rat,
but found he was too sly and quick for that.
Despite himself, he twitched his tail through all the dirt
he could and poked his little nose in till it hurt.
No sniff of sadness, no ripe morsel of dismay
escaped his rasping tongue, his earnest way
of making dark and disappointment his
next meal — for this was his perverted bliss.

Ballad of the Bundle

Why are you writing and writing,
why don't you hang up your clothes?
Tidying's just as rewarding as poems —
one might have supposed.

Send you to furbish the bathroom,
you stop at the basin taps
entranced by your own reflection,
riveted, utterly trapped.

Having a conversation,
you seem to be listening hard
and there is your writing hand creeping
to the back of an old Christmas card.

Rein-in this galloping impulse,
this urge to confess on the page —
look, I feel like a bee in a buttercup
drunk into desperate rage

by your boring, repetitive habit
of bringing me verses to read,
like a spaniel that's dug in the midden
for something that's long ceased to bleed.

GARDEN TOKENS
for Alison Paice
March 26th

Alison? Do you remember, Alison,
your gift of Garden-Centre tokens?
Well, today, a day of dazzlement
so warm it made us laugh, we planted out
four clematis: two whites, a pink
and a dark, blood-red. All on the arches
my brother welded-up for us: self-
colour steel that soon should rust.
Alison, perhaps you know about my eye?
Easier to think you do, than that you don't.
Easier to think you here, than gone.
Some souls seem more essential
to our keeping-on. About the eye—
I'd wear a patch for you. Black,
piratical—to make you swoon.
I can just see your Eric's face!
And here's a thing—I'm writing poems
by the bucketful—some almost good.
I find strange solace in internal rhyme,
as if to manufacture sense from what
is, after all, coincidence. Just as it was
that we could not prevent the way
you had to die— while I had merely
to propitiate the Cancer-God with one
unsatisfactory, jaundiced eye.

MARCH 27TH

Today, to SaffronWalden in the sun, although
the driving there through almost fog
unnerved my silent passenger somewhat—
a quality of silence like a flashing light
announcing *accident*. Not so. I drove,
for me, quite well. As we drew near, the sun
consented to come out, the morning cleared.
We trawled the various grades of shop
famed for their Charity: a favourite game.
Then, up Sun Hill to Reed's Emporium.
The girl, who we suspect inclines to men
in eye-patches, came off the phone to say hello.
Next, down to Kim's, now full and doing well,
for toasted sandwiches and cafetiere for two.

What else, the viewers ask? Why, nothing. Oh,
the Market, yes— one punnet of mustard cress.
You shake your heads. You think there must be
more? I'm trying out this part I've landed and
it's proving hard, you see, to get it right. True,
I'm not bumping into to things too much.
I've got the voice. Not quite exact— but, then
I'm not quite who I ever thought to be.

ARTIFICIAL-EYE DAY
For Hilary Wakeman

If the eye is the window of the soul, surely,
one will be enough— the gist of what you said.
So why this bricked-up, painted thing that stares
at me as if I'd spoken out of turn? The work
of Aliens perhaps? In fact the work of Shirley
in her downstairs den of eyes. Shame on me
for blind ingratitude. Shall I step you
through the day? Outpatients send me back
into the rain, across the shining tarmac to Rehab.
There you wait a bit for Jean to take you down,
via the lift, there seem to be no stairs, into a room
of children's games and toys and walls of children's
crayonings. There are no toys for grown-ups here.
A wall-chart of the eyeball shows what's gone.
Old Readers'Digest, Country Homes dumped
on the tired floor. Mismatched old chairs and then
hand-shake from the Lady of the painted eyes,
so soft you think you have imagined it. She sits
me down and takes a look—is unimpressed,
afraid the orb is still too fleshy underneath.
It needs to go back in, to shrink or else her work
will have a skyward tilt— and in the outer corner
there appears to be a small adhesion which also may
undo the proper fitting of the final eye—which
will not be for some months yet. Meanwhile
she'll fit a temporary. I never get to see her tray
of eyes: sorry, orbital prostheses. She goes
behind the glass-partitioned wall and picks a grey.
She bustles back and holds it next the other eye.
A lucky guess, she says and pops it in. This hurts.
I wonder how so soft a grip can hold it firm.

Four times she grinds and buffs it down.
To while the time between, I browse the Patients'

Charter in Bengali, Gujarati, Hindi, Punjabi, Urdu:
There's not much else to do. Rupert, self-satisfied, high
on the filing-cabinet's no chum to me: too taken-up
with puzzling-out the opaque stick-on hexagons
that shield the windows' lower halves. I do not tell him
he has missed the pair of starlings mating on the top-
floor's canvas canopies across the road. Soft toys
along the window-cill also ignore the silly stares
of such a two-dimensional bear. Strangely, a lovely
fuschia in a tiny pot glows deepest purple, softest white.
Jean, the one who brought me down, I learn, is celebrating
her last day at work—with work. How it is, from now on
 all appointments courtesy of Blackpool. Why?
Sighs and laughs. Shirley must grind on, alone.

Desultory, again my real eye ranges to a poster, stuck
half and half behind a floor-to-ceiling heating-pipe.
It's for the Eyeless Trust: the right-hand side too small
to read, the left, a picture of a mother picking up
her little boy. She smiles. His face tilts up, arms out,
hands wide. The caption reads *A beautiful picture
but Baby James will never see the love in his mother's eyes.*
Perched in my tatty chair, I want to bang my head and howl.
Could I have really—was it ever me who said, glibly inane,
the best antidote to your own is other people's pain?

Shirley stops whirring. Rinses the work, comes bustling.
Deftly, she dips and slips it in, holds up the glass.
My new eye looks at me without an ounce of empathy.
She tells me how to manage it. She says she'll see me
in one month. *Blackpool permitting, you mean*, I joke.
She smiles. She gives my hand the softest shake.

DREAM
March 29th

They've handed me this child
to be the child I've lost.
It's kindly meant
but can't be right.
Warily, it watches me.
I try a smile.
There's no response.
I try again.
When I look up, the social workers
have all gone.

We are alone.
Squatting down,
I take her firmly by the hands,
eye to eye.
That's better—
something gives—
and then I see
there is the image
of a crouching man
who, quietly, weeps.

A LETTER TO MY FRIENDS

My dears,
         The pain I'm in is self-induced,
the misery is likewise to be milked.
When we were young, remember how
we'd lend a friend a go of bubblegum?
Well, now I've got this lovely juicy strip
all to myself, and, being bored, I've chewed
and blown, and chewed and blown and buried
my silly face in it. Now all the flavour's gone,
along you come, I pull the gobful out and,
grandly, offer you the wretched half of it.

Having slammed about and yelled a bit,
having sprayed the walls and tagged the doors—
okay— having dumped it all on her,
then skulked away and scribbled it,
today he's feeling less outraged, less desolate.
Not good, but able to assess the part, seeing
the lead he thought he was—the Pirate
stroke hero stroke glamorous baddie—
has been written out. He's left with someone
merely slightly odd, which, since the same
might well be said of almost everyone,
makes him just on the cross-eyed edge
of everyday. New stance, new lines, new skills
of self-effacing presentation to be learnt.

While on his shoulder, fidgets still, the blurred
grey parrot of remembered sight.

Okay. It doesn't move, or just a smidgen to the left,
but, if I screw the lids and squint like Clint, it's good,
it looks the business. Colour's great. Although
my iridologist daughter says the constitution's wrong:
neurogenic not glycemic— silk not old string vest.
Still, she jokes, this might improve your general health.
Of course, when I get tired or am alone, engaging
with my looking-glass, the eye stares from the gaping
lids as if about to jump. I talk it down. I coax it in.
I sit the madman on my bed and offer him a drink.
You know, I tell him, you have to think how it might be:
things are looking up. *For some,* he says, *for some. Not me.*
Tell me—was it you who set my bloody parrot free?

This perfect boy

Watching you, fast-off, suckling your thumb,
so perfect, so untouched by anything of wrong,
I yearn to roll you up in bubblewrap,
to find a life-proof drawer to stick you in.

It can't be done, if only, little one, because,
awakened now, I see you watching me,
suckling on the grown-up thing that I,
your mad old Grandpa, have become

and so it is and so we know it has to be.
Behoves us then to be our better selves,
to show, in something like a decent light,
writ fair, the bits worth copying.

TO HAVE
April 2nd

To have breathed the cold breath of the moon,
to have seen her prance, new-coppered,
through the trees, to have this moment
to myself—

to have woken in the night to rain,
to have smelt the summer earth drink deep,
to have felt the wet tongue of the wind
on my bare skin—

to have been at all in this bright world,
to have held my girl, to have held our child
and now, her glad boy fast in my old arms,
is hold enough.

APRIL 6TH

Be careful what you unwish for:
considering all things, just be glad
the past's a locked and bolted door.

Unsay that word, settle that score,
undo all loves that made you sad?
Be careful what you unwish for.

No ticket back lets you explore,
as you are now, what you once had:
the past's a locked and bolted door.

No foresight could turn back that raw,
unfettered, bright-faced lad
with *careful what you next wish for.*

Could change of diet, staying poor
have stilled the cancer in the blood?
The past's a locked and bolted door:

you cannot be what once you were.
Though things go wrong, good comes of bad.
Be careful what you unwish for—
turn from that locked and bolted door.

April 8th
For Felix

Without, the Spring has come. Within, the trees
in my soul's walk stand stiff, unleaved.

Beyond the double-glass my single eye
spies sun and birds and butterfly,

but here, inside, I sit and nibble at the news,
served seasoned with its sly and partial truths—

and then you, waking, cry your help-me cry
and I rejoice at it. You see me now: your smile

slaps sunshine into my glad beating heart.
You laugh, hold out your arms. Spring starts.

April 10th
For Bundle

The tendency of love, to tend, to pretend,
the tenancy of care— you swear are not
your territory—

and yet you watch my every move
as one would monitor a child just up
and on his legs

and scoop me up when down I go
and tell me, yes it's terrible
but could be worse

and, growing into pain yourself
from daily fear and tiredness, nonetheless
you carry me—

and so, your territory's a crowded place
without a window to go by and see
your loving face.

SHELL CLEANING
April 13TH

Tonight, the eye looks waxy, dull and smeared:
a victim of unmeant neglect. I fish a plastic lever
from the pack, as though to change a fairy wheel,
to prise it from its coral bed into my hand.
It throws me one brief glance as if to say, *at last,*
then tips and slips into the sterile glass.
Un-eyed, the lids shrink back and muttering in,
mouthing phlegm as glutinous as vaseline.
I fill the eye-bath, give the mouth to drink.
It smacks its sore old lips. I flush it several times.
Now, moist as fresh-sliced ham, the socket gleams
and, lids stretched sideways, the adhesion shows
tethering the cobbled flesh at the eyeball's outer edge.
It has to go. I flush again with chloromphenicol.
Gingerly, I swill and rinse the weirdly profiled
plastic disc that counterfeits my blinded soul,
its secret thoughts. Bizarre. In that it stares
unflinching, sharp, it speaks me fair and well.
I slip it in and in a blink, I find I'm wondering
were it best to take its doubtful partner out?

APRIL 14TH

I'm half-blind
And you're half-deaf
But we're still dancing—
We ain't dead yet.
>Got our own teeth
>Got our own hair
>One or two brain cells—
>Don't despair.
You're half-mad
And I'm half-drunk
Or the other way round
But we ain't yet sunk.
>You'll see us there
>On the tennis court
>Tired old balls
>New bats new shorts.
Whoever steps first
Through the big black door'll
Hold it wide with
There's one more—
>But we're still dancing,
>We ain't dead yet
>Though I'm half-blind
>And you're half-deaf.
So, doh-se-doh
And swing me round
That cracked old fiddle
Has a sweet old sound.

CHANGING MY MARK
April 16TH

I've had this predilection since a boy—
romantic symbols— a yearning for the naf.
A silvered plastic Pegasus, a brooch: my
first shy Valentine, sealed in an envelope,
no card, no note, shoved through
the letter-box and gone. Thirteen I was.
And now I play the game again.
In hopeless love with my lost eye,
symbolically, I change my potter's mark.
With clumsy care I cut from flooring-tile
an Eye of Horus; test it as I go
by pressing it on blu-tack. Difficult
and not well done, but may suffice.

And now I see examining a mug thus marked
just here, beneath the handle as I do, the eye
stares back at me with sad, persuasive irony—
which pleases me. My prosthesis weeps.
I haven't stepped so far from that daft boy.
For posterity, on three tall flower-jugs
I make both marks: my old two-swans' necks,
used these forty years, and this Egyptian eye
to speak a new beginning and an end
of easy talk between my eyes and fingertips.

TRIUMVIRATE
April 17TH

Not simple this: there is the me who relishes
the standing-out; the eye-patch me.
And then the head-down me who craves
for nothing more than plain anonymity.
Me number-one blooms in this slight celebrity.
Me number-two, needs dull normality.

Not normal though this leaning at the sink
to pop your eye into your palm,
rinsing the sunk, repellent socket clean.
Just as it's hardly notable to bore
your glassy-eyed acquaintance with
your minute, coping strategies,
or how, despite the effort everyone has put,
you do things worse than once you could.

Not simply these: the patch-eyed peacock fool,
the anti-social grump. There is another me
grateful for my gentle bed, for love
that buzzes round me, honeying my hive,
for footing through the bubbling flowers
of this, my five and sixtieth spring.

Not normal, too, such privilege —
not to be starved, roofless, merely poor,
or tortured for belief or unbelief.
To have the wealth to send a cow,
or give a goat, whilst floating free
on my sweet cloud of luxury.
I've had one eye shut all my life —
so, what's this loss to give me grief?

GRAYSCALE
April 19TH

I have become convinced—convinced myself—
these grayscale patterns, which the brain projects
in lieu of my gone-missing eye, are fractal. Gorgeous
certainly and many-layered and shifting as a shawl
of silver silk hung in a half-lit, draughty hall.
Impossible to photograph or anyway record
and differing each time I close my eyes— the living
snowflakes of my dendrites and my axions. Once
only have I glimpsed them clearly in full light, briefly,
on a sun-white kitchen wall, like boiling gold. But, daily,
they are there, as blur of feathers by my irritated ear—
a voice that tells me nothing, ever, will be clear.

THE EYE UNIT: APRIL 20TH

It only needs one eye to see this is not
Sister's day. As bid, we're here at eight.
Plonked down at the reception desk,
she takes my letter, ticks the list
and waves us through to wait.
We riffle through the Hellos and O.K.s
that wear and tear their sad celebrity.
We settle for back-copies of New Scientist,
the which, I'm glad to say, we brought to dump.
A girl in scrubs soon comes to catechise.
Although I know it's only ticks on forms
it makes you feel you're in the swim,
not just abandoned, casually marooned.
An hour later, having checked the state
of play with the arrived receptionist,
we sally to the Concourse for a coffee-break.
As we go out I catch a glimpse of Woodruff
in his cutting blues, so, something's happening.
Returned, we sit the next hour out.
By now we have another couple of our age,
a robust carer with her wheel-chaired charge,
and a nice lady, an old hand, who's armed
with her book of puzzles: Sudoko. Inquiring
of Kelly, the girl-in-scrubs, I learn there's been
a hitch with the anaesthetist. Another hour.
As if from stage right comes a strong,
black-country voice, surprisingly attached
to a frail and emphasemic man, arm in breathless
arm with, I speculate, an equally myopic, lady friend.
They perch, half on their chairs, as if they quite
expect that they are next. By now I've ascertained
that I am third: two 'generals' from the ward,

then me. The rest are cataracts. Complaints
begin to grow like unwatched weeds. I tell them

117

what I know, then seek out Sister in the Ward.
Foolishly I say, *the Eye Unit is so efficient,*
normally—what's going on? She doesn't like it.
Nor would I. She tells me she has one nurse, not four,
eight bed patients, and day patients who, by rights,
should not be hers. She *is* efficient. Please just go
and wait. You will be called. Five minutes later
and she sticks me in a gown. Bundle, returning
from a further Concourse foray, asks, quite
loudly, if I'm done? This doesn't altogether help.
Like children failing to be good, we go and wait.

At half-past one, I'm chaired upstairs.
Mr. Woodruff, crisp, apologetic but unfazed,
explains that Admin. hadn't notified the required
anaesthetist, which set the whole works back
two hours. Addenbrookes, he says, too big.
The Eye Department's in five parts. Paperwork
falls down the cracks. Face swabbed with iodine,
eye drops to freeze, a speculum to gape the lids
and then the local needled in, four times.
This hurts. He tells me that I'm through the worst.
He sketches what he's going to do. Snip
the adhesion, draw down flesh to fill
the diamond gap that will result. I feel
hardly a thing. Four minutes, five—I'm done.
In recovery, the Theatre Sister chats and checks
me out. Suggests I tell the tale to PALS. At last,
they wheel me down, though I would rather walk—
But then, actual surgery apart, this whole day's
juddered, inexorably on: slow-motion as
a minor pile-up on a well-lit road: a lesson
in nothing-to-be-done, foot-down helplessness.

EIDOLON
April 27TH

Knowing there's nothing to be done
should make acceptance easier. Sadly,
my temperament is such that doing nothing
is the hardest thing. I need to find a way
to take the hinges off this nothing's door
if I can't simply kick it in—this Eidolon.

No way is this heroic—just the little boy
who banged his head on all the walls,
his mother crying in the hall.
I put my arms around myself, hold on.
Then I begin to reason with the child—
One, you are alive. The cancer, it would seem,
is gone. And left you with this lovely Eidolon.
The part of you they took away, the very part
you best could lose. Think if it had been a hand?
You can still manage everything you ever did.
Ok, not well, but well enough. You are still loved.
In fact, the gaping hole has overflowed
with kindness and surprising love. Come on,
come on—blow your nose. Sit up. Let's hear
no more of parrots or impossible grey Eidolons.

REMEMBER THEM?
April 30TH

Remember them, the dodgem cars, the sparks,
the jolting thumps, the screams, the brittle laughs?
A thing of youth, of boys and girls, of brown-faced men
with tattooed arms, who leapt from car to car
and kept you straight. Well, give or take the years,
the muscled arms, the summer dark, that's how it is
this Sunday lunchtime partying of largely passé
pensioners. Well-heeled but less well-sprung, the women
eye the men, who laugh, too loudly, in their little gang
and, raucous, welcome in the odd, bold girl who knows
there's little now to lose. No harm in this and, by and large
the girls still talk more real sense, of mothers who refuse
to die, of offspring still somehow attached, but best,
and with some joy at least, of children's children
growing tall, of life still opening its last flowers—

for us the dodgems have slowed down. The power
is intermittent but still there. The boys are still as boastful
and the girls yet take such trouble with themselves.
Quietly we stand and scream. Curbing our fear, we clutch
our glasses in our fists and wait the next big thumping jolt.
Some cannot see, some cannot hear, most cannot run.
Odd silences fill up with ghosts of everyday forgotten words.
Odd moments when we wonder who we're smiling at,
just who it was we have been talking to. Bright sparks
surprise us still, but they are few—though all of us
can sense each other's pain. Pain now the current
running through, to tell us we are still alive, to tell us
we still lean towards and dream and still, somehow, survive.

NOW WHAT DID I COME IN HERE FOR?
May 3rd

It gives me exercise, at least. At least
it gives me time to stand and stare at things
while the messengers upend their muddled bags
on the brain's unswept and littered floor.
I'm like a tourist in my life. All flights delayed,
I'm safely through passport control, unpinged,
into Departures. The most I seek from Duty Free
is brandy, cheap, with which to fight the frights
while I'm away with the faeries, as now, most days
I seem to be. Sometimes I look around for why
I'm where I am. Sometimes I fantasise
this is a lull in fighting: I turn to face the camera.
A few hours, days, years ago, I say, *it was all*
happening, right here, though where this is,
for reasons of security, I cannot rightly say—

Balloon Games

May 14th

We are playing balloons, can you see?
We sit on the floor, legs splayed,
batting the blue balloon between us.
The globe he bounces me's imbued
with mischief, joy and innocence.
The globe I send him back is tired
with love and greed and war,
with knowing ignorance. Forget
all that, just watch him now.
He tastes, he feels, he squeaks it
with his little fists, then squeezes,
chuckling as it flies and flirts away.
I catch it in my quick old reach.
It clings, full of his static.